UFO Crash Sites

by Dinah Williams

Consultant: Paul F. Johnston, PhD
Washington, D.C.

BEARPORT
PUBLISHING

New York, New York

Credits

Cover and Title Page, © tsuneomp/Fotolia, © John De Bord/Fotolia, © Byelikova Oksana/Fotolia; 4–5, © Kim Jones; 6, © Timothy J. Jones iPhoto Inc./Newscom; 7L, © Zack Frank/Shutterstock; 7R, © Alexey Stiop/Alamy; 8, © Richard Michael Knittle Sr./Demotix/Corbis; 9, © Courtesy Gene Fuqua/Blue Knights Texas; 10, © Ted Van Pelt/Flickr; 11, © Debra Jane Seltzer; 12, © geogphotos/Alamy; 13L, © Wikipedia; 13R, © James W. Penniston; 14, © Carri Yoak Simpson; 15L, © Alfredo Maiquez/Shutterstock; 15R, © Charleston Gazette; 16, © Pam Golding Properties, Grahamstown; 17, © yienkeat/Shutterstock; 18, © Sovfoto/Getty Images; 19, © ITAR-TASS/Sovfoto; 20, © Don Ledger; 21, © Courtesy of Cindy Nickerson; 22, © John Clift/Flickr; 23T, © S.E.T.I. (USA); 23B, © B J Booth/ufocasebook.com; 24, © Романвер/Wikipedia; 25T, © Paul Stonehill; 25B, © Photo courtesy of Lee Speigel, Huffington Post Weird News; 26, © Danita Delimont/Alamy; 27, © rook76/Shutterstock; 31, © Fer Gregory/Shutterstock; 32, © Natsmith1/Shutterstock.

Publisher: Kenn Goin
Editor: Natalie Lunis
Creative Director: Spencer Brinker
Design: Dawn Beard Creative
Cover: Kim Jones
Photo Researcher: Picture Perfect Professionals, LLC

Library of Congress Cataloging-in-Publication Data

Williams, Dinah (Dinah J.), author.
 UFO crash sites / by Dinah Williams.
     pages cm. — (Scary places)
 Includes bibliographical references and index.
 ISBN 978-1-62724-518-0 (library binding) — ISBN 1-62724-518-9 (library binding)
 1. Unidentified flying objects—Juvenile literature. 2. Human-alien encounters—Juvenile literature. 3. Roswell Incident, Roswell, N.M., 1947—Juvenile literature. I. Title. II. Series: Scary places.
 TL789.2.W447 2015
 001.942—dc23
                                   2014040714

For more information, write to Bearport Publishing Company, Inc., 45 West 21st Street, Suite 3B, New York, New York 10010. Printed in the United States of America.

10 9 8 7 6 5 4 3 2 1

Contents

UFO Crash Sites 4

What Happened in Roswell? .6

Alien Graveyard 8

Acorn Aircraft 10

Lights in the Sky 12

The Flatwoods Monster 14

Didn't Want to Believe 16

UFO or Meteor? 18

A Watery Crash 20

No UFO? 22

Amazing Artifacts 24

Photographic Evidence 26

UFO Crash Sites Around the World 28

Glossary 30

Bibliography 31

Read More 31

Learn More Online 31

Index 32

About the Author 32

Throughout history, people have seen unidentified flying objects (UFOs). Eyewitnesses living at different times and in different parts of the world have described glowing lights in the sky, disc-shaped "flying saucers," and even **aliens** who traveled within them. As far as we know, none of these UFOs have ever been **recovered**. Yet some have left startling clues behind when they have struck the ground.

In this book, you will visit eleven of the **eeriest** UFO crash sites. Among them are the scene of an explosion that knocked down 80 million trees, a hillside strewn with otherworldly **artifacts**, and the spot where the body of an alien pilot is said to have been found. As you explore each of these strange, out-of-the-way places, you will have a chance to decide for yourself whether or not a UFO really fell to the ground there.

What Happened in Roswell?

Roswell, New Mexico

On June 13, 1947, a New Mexico rancher named Mac Brazel heard a loud explosion during a storm. The next day, he made a startling discovery. On some ranch land, he found a long **trench**—as if a large object had hit the ground and skidded there—as well as a scattering of odd metallic objects. What happened afterward would lead to the most famous UFO case of all time.

The Roswell crash site

UFO CRASH SITE

UFO Museum - 114 N. Main - Roswell

Mac Brazel was puzzled by the strange trench and the objects that had appeared—seemingly out of nowhere. He gathered some of the material and reported his find to the local sheriff, who then reported it to officers at an Army base in nearby Roswell, New Mexico. On July 8, an army officer made a surprising announcement. He said that rumors of a "flying disk" being found in the area were true. The next day, however, the story changed. The army now said that the wreckage was just the remains of a **weather balloon** that had crashed.

After those first few days, the story grew and grew. Several people later came forward and said that the army had secretly removed alien bodies along with the wreckage. Then many books and articles appeared, claiming that the U.S. government was deliberately hiding evidence of a UFO crash near Roswell. As a result of all the talk about a spaceship, aliens, and a government **cover-up**, the tiny town of Roswell became world-famous.

Today, Roswell is filled with sights that remind visitors of the 1947 event. Among them are a UFO museum, a UFO library, and streetlamps that look like alien heads.

The Roswell UFO Museum

Alien Graveyard

Aurora, Texas

On the morning of April 17, 1897, ten-year-old Charlie Stephens saw a cigar-shaped airship in the sky above the small town of Aurora, Texas. This was years before the first airplane was invented. Shortly afterward, news of the crash of a strange aircraft appeared in the local newspaper. Then other people came forward with more eyewitness accounts. Was the object that fell from the sky a UFO?

The Aurora Cemetery

In the newspaper article, Aurora resident S. E. Haydon wrote about how the strange airship slowed down and then crashed into a windmill. As this happened, there was a huge explosion and the airship broke apart.

Haydon's story did not end there, however. He also wrote that the body of the pilot was found in the wreckage. It was badly **disfigured**, but there was enough left to show that he was "not of this world." The article's last sentence stated that "The pilot's funeral will take place at noon to-morrow."

A Windmill Demolishes It.

Aurora, Wise Co., Tex., April 17.—(To The News.)—About 6 o'clock this morning the early risers of Aurora were astonished at the sudden appearance of the airship which has been sailing through the country.

It was traveling due north, and much nearer the earth than ever before. Evidently some of the machinery was out of order, for it was making a speed of only ten or twelve miles an hour and gradually settling toward the earth. It sailed directly over the public square, and when it reached the north part of town collided with the tower of Judge Proctor's windmill and went to pieces with a terrific explosion, scattering debris over several acres of ground, wrecking the windmill and water tank and destroying the judge's flower garden.

The pilot of the ship is supposed to have been the only one on board, and while his remains are badly disfigured, enough of the original has been picked up to show that he was not an inhabitant of this world.

Mr. T. J. Weems, the United States signal service officer at this place and an authority on astronomy, gives it as his opinion that he was a native of the planet Mars.

Papers found on his person—evidently the record of his travels—are written in some unknown hieroglyphics, and can not be deciphered.

The ship was too badly wrecked to form any conclusion as to its construction or motive power. It was built of an unknown metal, resembling somewhat a mixture of aluminum and silver, and it must have weighed several tons.

The town is full of people to-day who are viewing the wreck and gathering specimens of the strange metal from the debris. The pilot's funeral will take place at noon to-morrow.
S. E. HAYDON.

The newspaper story from April 1897

The next day, townspeople are said to have gathered at the Aurora Cemetery for the burial. It is also said that the remains of the ship were tossed into an old **well**. Since that time, many people have visited the town, hoping to learn more. However, a tombstone that once marked the grave has been stolen. The well was searched, but only traces of **aluminum** were found. The only proof of the crash is the word of the townspeople, all of whom are now dead.

Some say that the story was a **hoax**. They claim that S. E. Haydon wrote the story to create interest in Aurora. The town had been going through hard times and the report brought visitors to the area.

The alien grave marker

Acorn Aircraft

Kecksburg, Pennsylvania

On the afternoon of December 9, 1965, a giant fireball streaked across the sky. It was seen by people in six U.S. states and part of Canada. Less than two hours later, people in Kecksburg, Pennsylvania, reported that something had crashed into the woods there. What happened next is still a mystery.

The Kecksburg crash site

At 6:30 P.M., Kecksburg resident Frances Kalp called a radio station to report that a flaming object had landed in the woods near her house. When reporters arrived to investigate, they found that the state police and members of the U.S. military had already sealed off the area. Later, two different official stories came out. The police released a statement saying that they had found nothing in the forest. The U.S. Air Force put out a report saying that a **meteorite**—a natural object from space—had crashed in the woods.

However, witnesses told a different story. Local firefighters claimed to have seen an acorn-shaped ship, about 9 to 12 feet (3 to 4 m) in length. At one end was a wide band covered by a type of picture writing. Another witness said that he saw a similarly shaped object being brought into the Wright-Patterson Air Force Base in Dayton, Ohio. Then, years later, a worker at the base came forward and said that he had seen a strange-looking **craft** being inspected in a **hangar**. Had a UFO landed after all?

In 1990, the television show *Unsolved Mysteries* investigated the Kecksburg crash. They made a model of the acorn-shaped UFO that witnesses had described. Today, the model—known as the "space acorn"—is displayed in Kecksburg on top of a tall pole.

The model of the acorn-shaped UFO

Lights in the Sky

Rendlesham Forest, Suffolk, England

In 1980, several members of the U.S. Air Force who were based near Rendlesham Forest claimed to see lights flashing through the night sky. Some of the servicemen thought the flashing lights came from a UFO. One man even claimed he was able to touch the object. Now, more than 30 years later, people are still trying to figure out what happened in the dark forest in England that night.

The Rendlesham crash site

At 3:00 A.M. on December 26, 1980, U.S. servicemen spotted bright lights over Rendlesham Forest. A patrol was sent out to investigate. Reports differ on exactly what happened next. According to Lieutenant Colonel Charles I. Halt, an object that had colored lights was hovering in the sky. As the men got closer, the object disappeared through the trees. Sergeant Jim Penniston, however, says he got close enough to touch the warm metal on the outside of the UFO before it took off into the sky.

In the morning, the servicemen returned to the site of their mysterious encounter. What they found amazed them. Three small **depressions**, which together would form a large triangle, were on the ground. The branches of nearby trees were broken and burned. Although investigations have continued since that time, no one can agree on—or explain—exactly what or who left these traces behind.

The Orfond Ness lighthouse

A drawing of the UFO made by one of the servicemen

Some believe the lights seen by the servicemen were from the nearby Orfond Ness lighthouse. At the time, Orfond Ness was the second brightest lighthouse in all of England.

The Flatwoods Monster

Flatwoods, West Virginia

On the night of September 12, 1952, a group of boys in a small town in West Virginia saw a fiery light streak across the sky. It appeared to crash by the neighboring Elk River. The boys got Kathleen May—the mother of two young brothers in the group—and some other friends and then rushed over to investigate. What they found both puzzled and frightened them.

Near the Flatwoods crash site

Kathleen May, her two sons, and their friends hiked through the foggy night to the crash site. There they found a huge blazing red light. A sickening mist burned their eyes and noses. When they saw two blue lights, they turned their flashlights toward them. Suddenly, they were able to see an alien! Nearly 10 feet (3 m) tall, it had a face that Kathleen May later described as being shaped like "an ace of spades." The lights came from the creature's eyes. It hissed and glided toward the group, then headed toward the large red light.

The group ran back to town and told their terrifying story. In the next few days, it turned out that other residents had also noticed strange things, including bright lights and terrible smells.

When investigators visited the site, they noticed the smell as well. There were skid marks where a large object appeared to have landed. However, there was no further sign of the creature—which has become known as the Flatwoods Monster. No one has seen it since.

U.S. Air Force investigators had a different explanation for what the group in Flatwoods saw. They believe the fiery light and burning smell were caused by the crash of a meteorite. The alien was a barn owl in a tree—which created the impression of a head on a tall body.

Kathleen May with a picture made by an artist to show how the alien looked

Didn't Want to Believe

Fort Beaufort, Eastern Cape, South Africa

Over the years, many UFOs have been spotted over the Eastern Cape of South Africa. In 1972, the skies above the area were especially busy. More than 20 mysterious flying objects were seen, often by a number of different people. According to eyewitness accounts, one alien spacecraft even landed near a sheep farm in a town called Fort Beaufort.

Near the Fort Beaufort crash site

Sheep farmer Bennie Smit didn't want to believe in UFOs. Yet after the events of June 27, 1972, he didn't have much choice. Smit went into the **bush** that day, searching for his farmhands after they had not come to work. When he found them hiding in a shed, he also saw what had frightened them—a glowing UFO in the sky. Smit had someone call the police and then went to get his gun. He shot at the craft several times but could not damage it.

Two police officers arrived, and one of them also began shooting. The drum-shaped, three-legged UFO landed in the nearby woods. Smit offered to go and investigate. He got within 50 feet (15 m) of the craft. Then it rose into the air and changed colors from green to yellow to white as it flew away.

Evidence of the visit included chunks of a concrete **reservoir** that exploded as the craft reportedly flew over it. Deep imprints of the spacecraft's legs were later found in the ground. Plus, five eyewitnesses, including Bennie Smit, all swore they saw the same UFO.

Bright, pulsing lights in the night sky are often thought to be UFOs but are later shown to be **meteor showers**. Yet not all sightings are so easily explained. On January 27, 2006, more than 20 people in rush-hour traffic near Cape Town, South Africa, reported seeing several UFOs. The bright white spheres—which were not meteors—remained in the sky for nearly ten minutes before flying away.

A meteor shower

UFO or Meteor?

Tunguska, Siberia, Russia

On the morning of June 30, 1908, in a remote area of southern Siberia, a huge and mysterious fireball was seen streaking across the sky. Some say it was almost as bright as the sun. Minutes later, a blinding flash lit up half the sky. Then there was a gigantic explosion. Were these events caused by a UFO crashing to Earth, the rock in a **meteor** blowing apart in the sky—or something else?

The Tunguska crash site

The massive blast that struck Tunguska, Siberia, more than 100 years ago was as powerful as 185 **atomic bombs**. It knocked over 80 million trees, which covered an area of 800 square miles (2,072 sq km). The explosion even threw one man out of his chair while he was sitting on a porch 40 miles (64 km) away. He said it was so hot at the time that it felt like his shirt was on fire.

Because the Tunguska region is so difficult to reach, the explosion was not investigated until 1927—almost 20 years after the mysterious event occurred. Today, scientists believe that a 220-million-pound (99,790,321 kg) meteorite entered Earth's **atmosphere** at 33,500 miles per hour (53,913 kph). The heat and pressure caused the space rock to explode in the sky and turn into a fireball that crashed to the ground.

Tunguska researcher Yuri Lavbin has a different explanation. He believes that a **comet** and a UFO collided, causing the enormous explosion. His evidence is two strange black stones found at the blast site. He claims they are the remains of an alien spaceship.

Yuri Lavbin

Some believe the remains found by Lavbin are parts from the *Vostok 1K* spacecraft. Launched on December 22, 1960, the craft came down in the Tunguska area. Many UFOs reported in Russia in the 1960s were later determined to actually be secret test runs of Russian spacecraft and missiles.

A Watery Crash

Shag Harbour, Nova Scotia, Canada

For years, the people of a small fishing village in Nova Scotia told spooky stories about ghost ships that appeared out of the mist, huge sea serpents that lurked below the water, and giant squids that swallowed people alive. However, on the night of October 4, 1967, some people were convinced that something incredibly strange had really occurred. A UFO had crashed into their harbor!

Site of 1967
← U.F.O. Incident

The Shag Harbour crash site

At first, the people in Shag Harbour thought that the strange orange lights they saw in the night sky were coming from an airplane that was crashing into the water. The Royal Canadian Mounted Police were immediately contacted. Yet no planes were reported missing. That's when investigators began to wonder if the lights belonged to a UFO.

Constable Ron Pound was one of many people who saw the unusual object over the harbor. He said the craft was about 60 feet (18 m) wide and had four flashing bright lights. After the craft hit the water, several officers rushed to the scene. They claimed to see a UFO floating about a half mile (.8 km) from shore. Yellow foam was trailing from the craft.

The next day, divers began searching for remains of the UFO, but nothing was found. It seemed as though the spacecraft—or whatever object was flying in the night sky—had sunk and disappeared forever into the cold, dark waters.

In 2008, the Shag Harbour UFO Museum opened. Each year, about 2,500 visitors watch television documentaries, read newspaper articles, and view objects related to the mysterious event that took place in the town more than 45 years ago.

UFO SIGHTING 1967

No UFO?

Llandrillo, Wales, United Kingdom

At first, it was thought to be a plane crash. Later, it was said to be an earthquake. Others claimed it was a meteor shower. Yet witness Pat Evans knows what she saw that night—a UFO.

Near the Llandrillo crash site

On the cold night of January 23, 1974, a number of people in the small village of Llandrillo heard a loud explosion. After going outside to see what had happened, they reported seeing strange blue and orange lights near Cader Bronwen mountain. It wasn't long before the ground began to shake. Shortly afterward, a local nurse, Pat Evans, received a call from the police. They wanted her help with what they described as a plane crash on the mountain.

Evans grabbed her medical kit and bundled her teenage daughters into the car. When she reached the mountain, she was shocked by what she saw— a large glowing orange craft. She and her daughters watched it for ten minutes before police and military forces near the object approached her. They told her she must leave the area immediately.

Pat Evans

Soon afterward, the roads were sealed off. No one but the military was allowed on the mountainside. Even shepherds were not allowed to come and take care of their sheep. The military claimed there was nothing on the mountain. Yet it was days before the roads were opened again. What were they investigating all that time?

Some believe that aliens died when their craft crashed on the mountain. Their bodies were supposedly transported to Porton Down, a military science center in Wiltshire, England. There is very little evidence to support this idea, but the rumor continues to this day.

A picture of alien bodies being removed, made by an artist

Amazing Artifacts

Height 611, Dalnegorsk, Russia

Whatever crashed into the lonely, **remote** hill known as Height 611 was not from this world. Scientists who studied the remains of the object are puzzled by where they came from. Some of them believe they are pieces of a UFO.

The Height 611 crash site

On January 29, 1986, residents of a small mining town in Russia noticed something in the night sky. A glowing metal **sphere**, approximately 10 feet (3 meters) across, was quietly flying **parallel** to the ground. As it neared Height 611, it made a jumping motion. The craft then fell onto the hill with a soft thud and burned in a strange blue flame for an hour. The impact caused a two-minute interruption of radio and television broadcasts.

Two days later, UFO researchers arrived at the crash site. The spot where the craft had burned now smelled of chemicals. Pieces of a silvery metal, some in the shape of little balls, were found on the ground. They were made of a mixture of iron, lead, and silicon, combined with other unusual metals. The odd substance was said to have **antigravitational** properties.

Some of the pieces of metal that were found

Also collected from the site were tiny nets. Scientists found they were woven with **microscopic** threads made of metals, including gold. This was very strange, for the technology did not exist at that time for the super-strong nets to have been made by humans.

Some of the material found at Height 611 can now be found in the National Atomic Testing Museum in Las Vegas. The display is labeled "Authentic Alien Artifact."

Photographic Evidence

Cape Girardeau, Missouri

Reverend William Huffman was a minister at the Red Star Baptist Church in the small town of Cape Girardeau. In the spring of 1941, local police asked him to come pray at the site of an airplane crash. However, when he arrived, he was shocked by what he discovered. Not only wasn't it a plane that had gone down—the crash victims were not human!

Near the Cape Girardeau crash site

Reverend Huffman drove more than 10 miles (16 km) into the woods before he came upon the crash site. The police, fire department, and other government agents were already there. Nearby was a disc-shaped aircraft with strange writing on its side. Beside it were three creatures that had died in the crash. They must have been from outer space!

Supposedly, a photo was taken that night of one of the aliens, and it was seen many years later by Huffman's granddaughter. She described the creature as being small and hairless, with long hands and three fingers. It had large eyes and a small slit for a mouth. Its skin was covered in what looked like wrinkled aluminum foil.

Before he left the site, Huffman was sworn to secrecy. Yet when he arrived home, he had to tell his family. After that, the story of what happened that night spread. Now some people who study UFOs believe it is true. However, the photo mentioned in the account has never been found.

Since ancient times, many people have claimed to have seen aliens. The witnesses often described the creatures in much the same way as Huffman's granddaughter did—hairless, with large heads and eyes and tiny mouths.

UFO Crash Sites

Cape Girardeau, Missouri

A minister is witness to three aliens who died in a crash.

Kecksburg, Pennsylvania

Eyewitnesses describe seeing an acorn-shaped UFO.

NORTH AMERICA

Aurora, Texas

An alien killed in an 1897 UFO crash is said to be buried in the town cemetery.

Shag Harbour, Nova Scotia

Near a small fishing village, an unusual craft splashes into the water, leaving yellow foam in its wake.

Roswell, New Mexico

Wreckage from a UFO and conflicting reports about what happened spark worldwide interest in this crash site.

Flatwoods, West Virginia

A group of people follows lights into the woods and comes face-to-face with an alien creature.

SOUTH AMERICA

Atlantic Ocean

Pacific Ocean

Around the World

Llandrillo, Wales, United Kingdom

When a nurse rushes to the site of a reported plane crash, she finds a glowing orange UFO.

Tunguska, Siberia

Millions of trees are knocked flat by a huge explosion.

Arctic Ocean

EUROPE

ASIA

Rendlesham Forest, England

Members of the U.S. Air Force witness a UFO landing in the woods.

Height 611, Dalnegorsk, Russia

A UFO smashes into a hill, leaving otherworldly artifacts.

AFRICA

Fort Beaufort, Eastern Cape, South Africa

A farmer shoots at a hovering craft.

Indian Ocean

AUSTRALIA

N

W   E

S

Southern Ocean

ANTARCTICA

Glossary

aliens (AY-lee-uhns) living beings from another planet

aluminum (uh-LOO-min-uhm) a lightweight, silver-colored metal

antigravitational (AN-*tye*-grav-uh-TAY-*shuhn*-uhl) able to resist the force that pulls things toward Earth

artifacts (ART-uh-*fakts*) objects that are of historical interest

atmosphere (AT-muhss-fihr) gases that surround a planet

atomic bombs (uh-TOM-ik BOMZ) weapons that can set off extremely powerful explosions

bush (BUSH) an area where plants and sometimes small trees grow wild

comet (KOM-it) a natural object that travels through space and is made up of ice, frozen gas, and dust

constable (KON-stuh-buhl) a title used for a police officer in Canada

cover-up (KOV-ur-UP) when people try to hide something or make it look as if it never happened

craft (KRAFT) a vehicle such as a boat, ship, airplane, or spaceship

depressions (di-PRESH-uhns) spots or areas that have been pressed down

disfigured (dis-FIG-yurd) changed or ruined by injury or some other cause

eeriest (EER-ee-ist) strangest; most mysterious

hangar (HANG-ur) a building where airplanes are kept and worked on

hoax (HOHKS) a trick that makes people believe something that is not true

meteor (MEE-tee-ur) a streak of light caused by a chunk of rock from space that burns up as it flies through Earth's atmosphere

meteorite (MEE-tee-ur-*rite*) a rock from space that has fallen to the ground

meteor showers (MEE-tee-ur SHOU-urz) groups of meteors appearing in the sky at the same time

microscopic (*mye*-kruh-SKOP-ik) able to be seen only with a microscope

parallel (PA-ruh-*lel*) running side by side

recovered (ri-KUHV-urd) found and brought back

remote (ri-MOHT) far away; hard to reach

reservoir (REZ-ur-*vwar*) a human-made lake that is lined with concrete

sphere (SFIHR) a ball-shaped object

trench (TRENCH) a long, narrow hole

weather balloon (WETH-ur buh-LOON) a large balloon that floats in the air, carrying instruments that send information about temperature, wind speed, and other weather conditions back to Earth

well (WEL) a deep hole dug in the ground to get water

Bibliography

Brooks, Philip. *Visitors from Outer Space.* New York: Doring Kindersley (1999).

Hepplewhite, Peter, and Neil Tonge. *The Unexplained: Alien Encounters.* New York: Sterling (1998).

Wilson, Colin. *UFOs and Aliens.* New York: Dorling Kindersley (1997).

www.ufocasebook.com

Read More

Krull, Kathleen. *What Really Happened in Roswell?: Just the Facts (Plus the Rumors) About UFOs and Aliens.* New York: HarperCollins (2003).

Owen, Ruth. *Aliens and Other Visitors (Not Near Normal: The Paranormal).* New York: Bearport (2013).

Pipe, Jim. *Aliens (Tales of Horror).* New York: Bearport (2007).

Learn More Online

To learn more about UFO crash sites, visit
www.bearportpublishing.com/ScaryPlaces

Index

Aurora, Texas 8–9

Brazel, Mac 6–7

Cape Girardeau, Missouri 26–27
Cape Town, South Africa 17

Dalnegorsk, Russia 24–25

Evans, Pat 22–23

Flatwoods Monster 14–15
Flatwoods, West Virginia 14–15
Fort Beaufort, South Africa 16–17

Halt, Charles I. 13
Haydon, S. E. 8–9
Height 611 24–25
Huffman, William 26–27

Kalp, Frances 11
Kecksburg, Pennsylvania 10–11

Lavbin, Yuri 19
Llandrillo, Wales 22–23

May, Kathleen 15

Orfond Ness lighthouse 13

Pound, Ron 21

Rendlesham Forest, England 12–13
Roswell, New Mexico 6–7

Shag Harbour, Canada 20–21
Smit, Bennie 17
Stephens, Charlie 8
Suffolk, England 12–13

Tunguska, Siberia 18–19

Vostok 1K 19

About the Author

Dinah Williams is an editor and children's book author. Her books include *Abandoned Amusement Parks; Haunted Prisons; Monstrous Morgues of the Past;* and *Spooky Cemeteries*, which won the Children's Choice Award. She lives in Cranford, New Jersey.